DADDY ISSUES

POEMS

J. R. ROGUE

J.R. Rogue
PO Box 984
Lebanon, MO 65536
www.jrrogue.com
contact@jrrogue.com

CONTENTS

For the fathers breaking cycles,
and the mothers filling both roles

CONTENT WARNINGS:

anxiety, depression, ptsd, suicidal thoughts, sexual abuse, physical abuse, rape, murder

HOW QUICKLY YOU FORGET

the cusp of fifteen—

I saw your ghost skin slip

by window & broken road

I am the bottom plate,

the dust on my brow,

the dazzling staccato

of my heartbreak

knit in my skin like deep red,

with no green to illuminate,

to lift that beauty

the cusp of often left behind,

the cusp of generations swallowing

the bait whole

I hope her laugh is a fright,

a shadow in the abyss when

you wonder where

the children have gone

"we were his children before these women"

your children, how quickly

you forget we are them,

we are we are we are your children

SPLIT YOU OPEN

you don't know

your naked body

beneath someone

new without

the drug,

the numb,

the anesthetic

they split you open,

devour your moans,

shy away from the cries

how is it different?

from the first time

a grown man touched

you when you were just a child?

YOU ARE WRETCHED FOR THE SHOVEL

how green the grass,

unfree, you are a prison

of your own making

when I called you from the fence

when I was but

a girl of six,

shoelaces peach

trying on shoes

like a leaver does

the fence denies me,

divides me in two

some part of me is with you—

& I cannot breath,

no the faint cry

through slats of wood I watch
grey hairs & mimics of me
under your adoring hand

I watch you create a life
that has no space for us,
& you are wretched for the shovel

I WAS NOT YET THE KNIGHT

he said he didn't like women

with tattoos, & I let it ride,

rode him into the night

like a stead,

like I was the knight

& I could save him

from stupid declarations

but I didn't even like him

his silly smile, & the way he said

it wouldn't be a thing,

but he wouldn't leave my

room in the morning

like I wanted

smiling & making dumb jokes,

the way I played at a smile,

& pet his dog, sent him into the heat

he said he didn't like women with tattoos,

& I paid another visit to the needle,

to the ebony lines

let the drama inside me prove

him wrong, proving myself a fool

for thinking I was proving anything

I said I didn't like him

but screamed into the woods

the day he pretended

he didn't know who I was when I texted

when he claimed

to be a different person,

wrong number,

who is this?

he said he didn't like to women

with tattoos,

& I let him ride into my dreams,

the ghost on a shelf,

the hollowed out space

I like to fit myself into

it doesn't matter

how he plays

I let it ride,

& I was not yet the knight

MANGLED MASTERPIECE

I am no preying,

no mirror image in

the manner of her

you hilt the knife,

marvel at the red,

the laugh caught there

you are so unlike her,

so cunning,

as that spite/light spills in,

gasoline to my ankles

like a bond we cannot manifest

lies like pages in a book

I am no preying,

no mirror image in

the manner of her

I am your failure,

your mangled masterpiece

I am wise to the deceit you grow

I am no mirror image

of the the madness you

make-believe in her

HOLLOW SPACES

remarried to the mar,

the mirror of horrors where

a father should be

the phone rings

& she hears lies,

chasing tides

& my feet have

been dry for years,

where were you

on the days my name

was supposed to be blue sky

like a daughter & father dance?

instead it was warning, curse on
your new wife's forked tongue—
the vile you let slide by

remarried to the mar,
the mirror of hollow spaces where
a father should be

10. he is dead

9. he is not in this room & he never can be

8. I've finally signed up for therapy so

maybe I'm going to survive this

7. two of my eyelashes

are sitting on the nightstand

6. I had a drink to have fun

not to get drunk, to feel numb

5. this is progress

4. I sat in the sun

3. sometimes you don't have to

finish what you started

10. he is dead

YOU MADE ME UGLY

I had to make peace

with the part of me

that wanted

a man to sleep far

beneath our

feet so that the secret

tapping against

my sternum could die with him

I had to make peace

with the part of me

that wanted cancer to win

when so many

are ruined by its

grip every minute

I had to make peace

with the part of me

that I was not born with

that he planted in me

when he looked

at me the way grown

men shouldn't

I had to make peace

with the part of me that wanted

to sleep far beneath

your feet

so that the secret

tapping against

my sternum could

die with me

A BRIDE OR A BURDEN

no aisle walked,

no soft hand letting

me go to the next

I noticed the absence, you see—

no roof to shield me,

no kiss on temple—

skinned knees patted

with warm palm,

someone to stay,

it was not bred in you,

burned away by your

bitter offerings

"who was I whose own

a bride or a burden,

responsible for making

grown men turn to vapor

I noticed the absence,

you see...

SORROW BREEDS

wrists pinned

to crisp sheets

where

panic lives

salt crawling

to pillowcases

where

sorrow breeds

shame

grown in bones

where thieves whisper

away the pure bits

you were born with

my lover's love

will wash away

the stain of those

who deserve

no mention of

their name

A NURSERY RHYME FOR BITTER MEN

why did the little girl leave?

a nursery rhyme for bitter men,

I'll sing it true

all of eleven years old

& you pass

the blame like a bottle,

like a running ember

meant to blind my eyes

to all you thieved

was the next

women the best?

the rest?

the place you needed to hide?

do you know who I am

I am not my mother,
but your blame lands
like a knife deftly thrown,

open palm holding
no forgiveness,
just shame & blame

why did the little girl leave?
why would she stay?

SLIGHTS OF OTHERS

my heart is not as hardened

as they hoped, the wall around

this muscle decays with age,

& I imagine loving you

I imagine a hug, warm eyes

I imagine the past left there

I will not allow arrows

to pierce my heart for the slights of others

I am my own woman,

my own vessel

I am not the punching bag

for the sins you saved for her

my heart is not as hardened

as they hoped, but it is wary

still capable of an open door

until the grave calls you home

DIRTY, BLOODY, MARROW
JANUARY 10, 2015

do you want the truth?

the dirty, bloody, marrow of me?

Eternal Sunshine

of the Spotless Mind

is a load of shit

the worst event in my life,

the moment I can't break free

from defining me,

occurred somewhere before

the age of nine

it's gone

I don't remember

& the truth is, the scars
don't go away

they're permanent
even when the memory
too
forgets you

THE GRAVE HAS LONG FINGERS

I see you in my face,

in the mirror

in the color of my hair,

in the tremor of my mother's voice

when she says

I look just like you

you are gone,

the grave has long fingers,

greedy hands

the motherland took you

back like a crack—

it gobbled you up,

& my mother's hands
have nurtured me

I am frozen at five,
breaking open three years ago
when you said my name,

did you know it was
not far away?
the retreat?

the grand finale out of a life
you never wanted?

I am a broken heart,
an open wound

& if I had been a boy,
would there be a poem
in my throat about
the way you faded away?

CORPSE
MAY 12, 2016

I spilled everything to my lover,

at 2:21 AM knee deep

on a hot July night,

on a hand-me-down mattress

in the shitty double

wide my uncle

let me crash in, while he served yet

another sentence in prison

I dressed in a

straitjacket night

I would bury the *father*

who killed all the

pretty posies in me

nothing would stop me

I spilled everything

to my pillow,

at 2:21 am knee deep

on a cool August night,

on a brand new pillow top mattress

in my pretty new house

while my lover stayed away,

    because I had already crucified

him for asking

    me one simple question

"what happened to you?"

ON THE DOWN SLIDE

magic man, never a moment

when you are not making

music of lies, making moments

disappear into hot cars,

steamed tears,

cunt chasing, car crash villain

you are the villain

& this is not the villain's story,

the tale of the dark hero

lets not romance this

you are the disease,

the forked tongue

you are the amber you drink

& the aching head
to glass the next morning

five feet up feels nice
& kind on the down slide

magic man, never a moment
when you're not making
more muscle down threats,
a heart break chasing a car crash
daddy disease

OUR RED BOND

broken wall, bloody fingers,
ripping away like red
on the floor

you breed that which
you do not bow to,
that which you do not know

I am a shadow
on your wall,
white crisis like

the clean slate
you could never conjure

the rain-checks pile up,

flooding the lawn,

the house,

the walls high

as hours spent

clocked in, out of our lives

doting husband, disdain lingers

ripping away our red

bond as dust collects on the floor

the clean slate

you could never conjure,

I attempt as

broken records

play,

a brazen life lived new

CONSTANT, & UNMOVING
APRIL 30, 2015

my heart turned black two

& half years ago when

my mind reminded me that

not all daddies love their

little girls the way they should

it's been so long since I've fallen

into anything other than this dark

since I've been exposed

I don't let myself,

because the only thing

that will hold me is this ache

I'll let you undress me,

but this loneliness,

I'll always wear

can you bear it still?

I suppose this is me breaking—

moments of stillness between

waves of insanity

we've both traveled far

past the point of hoping for the better

why you're standing there,

hands in your pockets,

digging your toes in the sand,

constant, & unmoving,

letting me crash, burn,

& drown you,

I'll never know

LOST LEAVING NOTES

no blood to bind,

& you face away like

wind on the soil

I do not know how

to make myself your flesh,

your shadow, wide eyes,

& wondering at why

I am never enough—

the shower holds my salt,

my assault on my face

in the mirror

why try?

why cry to fogged windows

& lost leaving notes

I sketch your new family
in the black of paper thicker
than our bond,

thicker than soil &
the wind of your leaving
skating across it like

wide eyes & expired tears

SURFACE FLOATING
MAY 4, 2015

surface floating sounds

pretty pretty

it paints a

posy perfect picture

but it's not

I've been surface floating

nearly three years now

my life looks

hazy down there

below

the paper me plays my part

I give her a passing grade

& most don't notice I'm

not present behind my pupils

THINLY WRAPPED FALSEHOOD

shiny wrapped gift

in a hand I cannot hold,

you are weak of mind,

easily poisoned,

easily positioned on the battle

field facing this side

the side you once loved,

broke bread with,

created life with

are you so weak willed?

so easily swayed?

what gift could

I buy your love with?

thinly wrapped falsehood
in a hand I cannot lift
you doll out love to those

with the grey,
walk away from life so young,
ready to grow

DECAYING WITH EACH REBIRTH

I can see your shiny shoes,

cufflinks, handsome face

braking bread

with white teeth,

money fat in the

wallet like a tick—

vices are blood red

I can hear the sound of the chopper

that took you away to save

the life you seemed

begging to break open

the weeks

became memorized

moments,

movement to places

I could not follow

a daughter is no vacation,

no blazoned emblem

on your shirt,

no status symbol to guzzle down

that hungry gullet like a mouse

I can see your shiny pills,

swollen heart in all it's wrongness

small chunks decaying with each rebirth

the sound of the life you preferred—

like your designer clothes

& days away

I will not follow

A BONE DEEP NUMB
JULY 1, 2015

I bruise easy

everything is pear-shaped

I put my feelings in a jar

easy extraction

tell me how to feel?

everything I paint is grey

black frames, art eyes,

& a bone-deep numb

his blood will take his side

LESS MONSTER, MORE MAN

a warm yellow light on the wall,

beautiful color like the

feeling we have parted

does the high fill you up?

does the burn make you fly?

they cannot turn back time,

the young girls you date,

you are still stuck in this—

failure or father?

you cast a wide net,

pull them to your side of the shore

I am warm yellow,

fading tide like the lies

I cannot swallow

he is husband,

growing parts of him

that you annihilate,

gun down with casual indifference,

racist nicknames tossed over

where is the gun that stole me?

where are the years

I said *daddy* to my kidnapper?

did the high fill you up

when you sold sister, daughter?

the fame you write

cannot turn back time,

cannot make you

less monster,

more man

SLEEPING WITH THE LIGHTS ON
OCTOBER 27, 2016

cut me open & shape me into

something that

maybe *maybe* makes sense

I road tripped down south with

the ladies who have my heart,

checked into a dirty hotel,

holed up some nights,

painted the boardwalk the rest

I drew a line in the sheets

so they couldn't touch me

then stumbled into a stranger's

bed the next morning

I can take the touch of a man

who doesn't love me

but I'll shrug out of an

embrace that lasts

too long with those

who know

my deepest

sleeping with the lights on,

throwing a bone to the villains,

letting them under my covers,

scaring the heroes away

I'm not sure they would

want to stay anyways

I WILL SHINE WITH LOVE

he is no shadow,

he is no nameless

he wears the name father

like a badge of honor,

one you threw in the dirt

I am no bill to pay,

no long letter to write

explaining away all the ways

the world has left you crippled & lacking

he is no shadow,

& I will shine

with love you couldn't pull forth

BUT I AM STILL SCARRED

stitched lips, silent eyes

assessing the damage,

brick wall heart

& I break myself upon it,

feel the steady edges,

I needed different, not more

mind open like a siv,

heart open like a well

I fell in, broken life like

waves on the shore

I wish I had known more,

but you were the mirror,

& I stitched these lips in kind,

in retribution,

in memoriam

I love you, I love you,

like a pair to the unknown,

there is worse,

I know this,

but I am still scarred,

still scared of the ways

I will hold this silence

like a second lover

father, I wish I had known more

I wish you had said so much more

I WAS THE ONLY ONE
APRIL 12, 2015

I couldn't hide from the moment

snap

flash

process

it's real

it's here

there's proof

I had big brown eyes

I was the only one

I had a strange last name

I was the only one

I never understood

not until I found that worn

out polaroid in the shed

I was dodging wasps &

pretending I was April O'Neal

I wasn't looking to find

big brown eyes, so like

my own

shared with a man

who gave me my strange

last name, & nothing else

I GREW FROM DIRT

mirror mirror, I love the

way you've cracked,

shown me the hardened parts of me

that match the hardened parts in you

I was a wish never wished,

a lineage never watered,

but I grew from dirt

& desperate pleas

for a life alone

you are the voice on the line,

the call I make,

the shattered glass

of a ceiling covered in grey

mirror mirror, I love the
way you've cracked

"I suppose I love him
& hate him in a similar
way that I love & hate myself"

THIS COUNTENANCE

draw a line down the center,

you aim at the board,

lined up like a soldier,

like family is a war

when all I knew were things

little girls should not,

how she was raped—

the beast who fathered

pushed you into the dark,

the more I grip,

draw a line down

the center,

the more the winter brings

drunken nights,

& who do you see here?

on this countenance?

how do you see the smile

you have let die?

when the power is cut,

when the water will not run

will you still cling to this old regret?

you were not there first,

but could have been there last—

a man's violent pride

is the beast we cannot tame

FIVE MINUTE FATHERING

my mendings

are white anew,

black & broken phone lines

the letters on pages worn

under fingers that know

too much of leaving

recover this morsel

of war in my chest

the time-clock ticks

on your five minute fathering,

your job well done

& your absence

benefits the whispers

my mendings are white & new,

like scar tissue

& broken connections,

phones pleas lost to time

& circumstance,

too much of leaving

SPIT IN LIKE AN INSULT

love *love*,

I wanted a war,

a monument to love,

a burning of cities,

a cuffing, & red,

& blue lights as you took

his life for what

he did to me—

is this not what a father does?

life for a life—

mine is still blinking,

& he is left alive

& no one knows of the taking

love for six years old,

for fences jumped

& innocence ripped

you shy at the tear,

deny the scar tissue beneath

thick & lumpy,

lacking empathy,

spit in like an insult

I wanted a war,

a monument to love,

but I got you

I spend too many
nights braiding
the hair of a
daughter
I can never give you

NO GRAVE FOR YOU

ghost—no grave for you,

long black parts of my

heart still ache for an embrace,

enough of enough to make

you want to stay,

want to be a mirror,

a hand on the ledge,

open mouth of wisdom

I have barred the bay,

iron cages keep out luck

& losing you over

& over like a

memory I cannot shake

the drink is common lover,

common thief

stealing the nights

the years have

become decades,

the forgiveness still worn thin

you cannot take from

these sons I have birthed—

the mirror images of all you never

wished to kiss of brow

CHOKEHOLD

where does the rage go?
the hate?
your demons got
you in a chokehold,

poured gasoline over our love—
your heart couldn't take it,
knocked you out cold,

& I am cold, colder,
courage shrunk up &
smaller when I speak

I loved your laugh,
hated the cheat,
the pills,

the rifling hands though

wallets & drawers

aching for that next fix

where did the life of the party go?

slurred speech & nightmares,

the moon got you in a chokehold,

witness to all your wild wrong,

the way you let them speak close

with warm breath, friends in name,

I hated their laugh,

loved yours

smaller when I speak this,

braver than I allow

myself to hold

A PARADE OF CLOWNS

a parade of clowns,

but I do not laugh

at the way they abuse you,

use you,

& flip mirrors like knives

I am the damage,

the collateral discernment

why do I cry for

your mother wound?

your deep red that

feels like salt,

taste like pennies & pennies

& pent up me is

opening on the dawn

I can break this cycle,
this round & round
to the sound of my healing

BLIND DAUGHTERS

I beg the question to

the bathroom mirror,

wipe it away when he steps

from the steam

you have left that here,

in the forgotten parts of my heart,

a yearning for love

when love is a fading memory,

when it is spat & underfoot

you begged the question

from my mind when

you flittered & ghosted

out of our lives

blind daughters—

mute moments

we cannot break free,

grasping for a

measly sliver of love

& you have left nothing here

I HOWL INTO THE NIGHT

the daughter of wolves,

the howl in the night,

& this sliver of

resistance is not enough

I reject your hand,

your warm embrace,

& this of all others

this is not the knife

I thought it would be,

not the wall I could proudly erect

you made me this way,

left me to fend for myself—

the daughter of wolves

armor anchored

in my own womanhood

I howl into the night,

but never your name

WHEN YOU DIDN'T HAVE TO

I found a picture of you,

a worn tan box &

your mustache

I felt nothing when I saw your face

I felt no rage, no anger,

no disgust

it is a numbness

I have pulled tight,

a second skin

I was there for your wedding

I ran away from

home to live with you—

though I knew you were bad father,

bad boyfriend,
bad husband

I knew,
& then it was all I knew

the man who shares this mane,
these black eyes,
he was never there,

& that is a wound that
will never be as deep
as the one you gave me

deeper than flesh,
buried in my heart
I remember your
racist comments

the way you calmed
a wild beast
putting holes in the
ceiling of
our trailer from miles away

the trailer you left us in—

second family, when we
were supposed to be the first

I remember pushing my peas
around on my plate,
you dressing up as
Michael Myers to scare us

bloody stump games
in the living room

how can I have these memories?

laughers & happiness—
abandonment & a shame
I can never wash off,
no matter
how many years
you have been dead

I found a picture of you,
& I didn't throw it away,
not at first

but when I found it again,
I threw it in the trash

I felt nothing

& you feel nothing
& they think I am
bad daughter,
the ungrateful

all you did for me
when you didn't have to,
& I didn't see you
in the hospital as the
cancer wasted you away

I did once,
cried as I cry
while writing this

I loved you

I loved you when
you didn't deserve it
not even your own flesh
& blood wants
to carry that name

I think of reaching

through states,

to a cousin who is not a cousin

did the drugs rip forth

from this?

the infidelity?

when we were kids she told me

you weren't my father

did she wish you weren't her uncle

when you touched her?

I loved you

how can you love a monster?

how can you shower tears,

drown the drain with salt,

when so much was taken?

THESE NEVERS

I watched tears,

rainwater on window,

salt on cheek,

the boldness of your shoulder,

your arm as you ripped

the phone from the wall

the never king,

the shadow I flinch at

I watched my life be

adopted by others,

salt on cheek,

but your presence black

the never king,

the crown

I wear

your ghost was the gift

ALLEYS

I can hear the choppers

when I close my eyes,

feel the rush of wind

as I ran down alleys

& open fields

you are a ghost,

a mess of a man

I wish I did not love—

did not share blood with

running legs, running tears

when I close my eyes

A REFLECTION

would you have stolen me away?
like dreams & naps in the car,
like the stranger at the airport
who eyed me like a prize?

would I have loved them?
grandfather & mother
I do not know

they never reached out, did they?
did they throw
me away in their hearts,
lock doors, such as you?

I hope those who wear
your name do it with pride—

I did, such pretty a word,

& I knew no one with it

magic is what kids dream,

& I thought I made it on my own,

my own name full of beauty

I wonder, if I had been Johnathon

who I would have been to you

would I be deeper image

a reflection she could

not look away from?

would you have stolen me away

so he never stole from me

this innocence you never got to see?

DREAD MEMORY

you were supposed

to be the shield,

the hard voice that

scared monsters away

but you break bread with,

love, share blood

with the brother who touched

me & took stark innocence away

I am white wall,

no clean slate,

but I stare at the red of my

mangled shadow

you were supposed

to be the shield,

you are dread memory,

dream horror

the voice that

loves my taker,

my monster,

my abuser

anyway

BURN YOU FROM VEINS

the rustling of leaves,

the warring words—

my love on your

face like a shield

how could you touch them?

sister to me, no blood to you,

as if the word incest

was too far,

as if what you let

loose on them

was nothing more

than an ignorance,

a slip of the hand

what stories you tell,

what lines they gobble up

I am unable to burn

you from veins,

goad you out of shadows

in my mind like a sin

I am not half monster,

my lost love on your face like a prison

how could I love you now?

DAUGHTER OF NO ONE

my best features stolen

from a man who

wears my name—

gave this name

& knows not

my voice,

my hopes,

the scar on my leg,

& the freckles anew

a man who is not

a man sometimes,

forever branded

for mistakes made

when he was half my age

mistakes I'm not sure

I care to hollow out,

splay open—

knife to the gut

like the heathen I am

my worst features start

at that hollow on my face,

they zero in,

the crease of brow,

the foreshadow

of a cry in the day,

the hollowed

out tree of my throat

his best features give me a

wink in the mirror,

battle with the wrinkles

I shed in my dreams

I am the wolf, black hair,

black eyes—

I am the wolf

daughter of abandon

daughter of no one

DADDY DADDY DADDY

who would you be if
I could give you what
you wanted then?

a dark haired child,
dark eyes like us,
dark humor & short stature

your family name
& my warring ways

how deep would my
mother wound be?

how much would it have
hurt him or her—

blurring

into nothing like

we cannot

be this way

we are nearly forty,

& I have shot arrows,

dodged chains

who would you be if

I gave you what you wanted?

more than husband,

daddy daddy daddy

dark & dreamy—

grey hair & calm voice

you're everything

I looked for in them

calm brow,

& you never leave

you never leave,

the way they did

WONDERING AT GRAVES

why did you keep me from him?

what love would have

been broken open,

spilled forth?

I am no mother's daughter,

no memory you

can shove in the drawer,

sweep out in the night

who would I be if you

had let me love him?

I am wondering,

woken,

open to the feeling of hurt

I hold sand from his land,

hold stories in my head of

who we could have been

why did you keep me from him?

mother wounds fester,

I am wondering,

weeping,

wishing on past

days I cannot

rewrite

what would we have

said if I had made

that phone call?

I am wondering at graves,

sweeping tears

out into the night

A FOREVER SLEEP

you are rough hands,

taught neck,

a red the canvas

cannot capture

a sound a poem plucks,

no petals for me,

no soft landing for

this blood we share

eyes are black like night,

a forever sleep I wish to linger in,

to dream away in fantasy days

this familiar ache

is wandering,

wishing me away

to a life that

does not clutch close,

pull near

you are rough hands,

a well of hurt you will

not articulate

you cut down Time's tree,

& we see the rings,

the wounded way we carry on,

rough scars for the stars

too wrecked over

to recover

FOREVER THE CHILD

I am the child,

I say that in the mirror,

repeat my lines,

hope the lies you

made me feel fade,

& every morning

I am awake to the

breaking of glass,

the shutting of old dreams

in my echoing mind—

a knife to the heart

I am the oldest child,

holder of hate,

repenting reconciliations

unlucky 13 when

you danced on dawns

that would never repeat

I want to stop wondering why

I am forever the child

BREADWINNER

you smelled like cigarettes,

looked like a normal man,

slight & balding

& vain in so many ways

but a heart turned

black beat inside of you

sexist martyr,

racist shadow,

breadwinner,

chain placing fool

I will never

be like you

BE AS QUIET AS POSSIBLE

the grief is ugly; don't let them see

suffer in silence,

let your daddy issues be sexy

the joke you're in on

the red nighty,

the red lips

the fuckable girl

he met at the bar

the grief is ugly;

let it seep onto his skin,

let it push on his pores,

suffer in silence,

no one likes a *slut*

who can't stop crying

be as quiet as possible

they don't like the dance

they don't want

three-letter words

daddy issues

as if we are the issue

& not the dads who raped

& touched

& left

& beat their little girls

that girl has daddy issues

that girl wears grief so ugly

be as quiet as possible

when you condemn the man

he just wants a good life?

god, he got hoodwinked,

he got saddled up,

he got tied to

the ole ball & chain

the grief is blue;

don't let them see

be as quiet as possible
when you break the dam free

light as a feather,
sharp as a boardwalk

the red sundown,
the red lips

the forgettable girl at the bar
he won't bring home to mother

the grief is sticky,
let his melt into his skin,
bring him into the dance,
hold him close

he just wants a good life—
exorcise him from what's left of yours

ACKNOWLEDGMENTS

Thank you to all the wonderful readers who submitted their stories. Thank you for letting me write for you.

J.R. Rogue first put pen to paper at fifteen after developing an unrequited high school crush and has never stopped writing about heartache. She has published multiple volumes of poetry and novels. Her work has been recognized with three Goodreads Choice Awards nominations, a testament to the impact of her work on readers.

In addition to her writing, J.R. Rogue is a certified yoga teacher with additional certification in Yoga Nidra and Trauma-Informed Yoga. She is passionate about mindfulness and meditation and is studying Foundations in Meditation. Furthermore, J.R. Rogue has been sober from alcohol since January 1st, 2020, a personal achievement that she is proud of and that has strengthened her commitment to mindfulness and wellness.

J.R. Rogue resides in a small town in the Midwest with her family, where she enjoys a peaceful life reading and telling stories.

You can find important links and information here. Join her mailing list to keep up with everything she's working on.

<u>www.jrrogue.com</u>
<u>contact@jrrogue.com</u>

instagram.com/authorjrrogue
threads.net/@j.r.rogue
facebook.com/jrrogueauthor
tiktok.com/@jenro501
amazon.com/J.-R.-Rogue
bookbub.com/authors/j-r-rogue
pinterest.com/rogueauthor

ALSO BY J. R. ROGUE

Romance

MUSE & MUSIC SERIES

Breaking Mercy

Burning Muses

Background Music

Blind Melody

SOMETHING LIKE LOVE SERIES

I Like You, I Love Her

I Love You, I Need Him

I Like You, I Hate Her

Romantic Suspense

RED NOTE SERIES

The Rebound

The Regret

The Return

Supernatural Suspense

OZARK OMENS SERIES

The Girl Next Door

STANDALONE NOVELS

Kiss Me Like You Mean It

POETRY

GOODREADS CHOICE AWARDS NOMINEES

The Exquisite Pain of the Unrequited

Exits, Desires, & Slow Fires

I'm Not Your Paper Princess

Tell Me Where it Hurts

Dark Mermaid Song

Songs for the Stars

After The Blackout

I'll Be Your Manic Anxiety Queen

Daddy Issues

The Words I Wish You Heard

LETTERS FOR THE UNIVERSE

Poems for the Moon: Vol 1

Poems for the Moon: Vol 2

Poems for the Stars: Vol 1

Poems for the Stars: Vol 2

Poems for the Dawn: Vol 1

Poems for the Dawn: Vol 2